LET US HAVE A GOOD DAY!

COVID-19

~~~~~~~~~~~~~~~

Jolene McCall

Let Us Have... A Good Day
COVID-19
Copyright © 2020 by Hori-Son Press

All rights reserved. No portion of this book may be reproduced, stored in a retrieval system, or transmitted in any form or by any means electronic, mechanical photocopy, recording, or any other except for brief quotations in printed reviews, without the prior permission of the Publisher or Copyright Owner.

Cover Art by Lynn H. Pellerin

ISBN 978-1-938186-06-6

SAN 920-251X

Throughout this book, the name satan has deliberately not been capitalized. To capitalize a name would be proper grammar, and it also shows respect to that person. Since, I have no respect for satan or any demonic force of that nature, I choose to be grammatically incorrect and refrain from capitalizing his name.

"Scripture taken from the New King James Version. Copyright © 1982 by Thomas Nelson, Inc. Used by permission. All rights reserved."

"Scripture quotations marked (ESV) are from The Holy Bible, English Standard Version® (ESV®), copyright © 2001 by Crossway, a publishing ministry of Good News Publishers. Used by permission. All rights reserved."

King James Version (Crown copyright/Public Domain in the United States)

Acknowledgements

To my Heavenly Father,

Thank you, Lord for Your blessings that you continue to pour into my life! Even when I have not deserved your mercy and grace, it has always been there—You are the Alpha and Omega, the Beginning and the End; You are my Light in utter darkness, the One that I call upon who shall never leave nor forsake me! Your unending devotion in my life shall always lead and guide me through the good and the bad—I shall never want for more but shall always desire that my eyes see You clearly, my ears hear Your voice—throughout my days, let them be filled with Your presence that I not only see and hear truth, but that my whole being is awakened to your presence within—as I feel your gentle touch, taste the goodness of your ways, and smell the freshness of a world to come! Be the light among darkness as only You can bring forth the illumination to our senses, and it is in You that we shall trust!

Dedication

This book is dedicated to my second grandchild, Charli. I have often referred to my granddaughter, Charli, as my "little oak tree." From the time she came into this world, I knew she was special.

There was a saying by an unknown poet, "The mighty oak was once a little nut that stood its ground." As I read that saying many years ago, I thought of you. You are my little nut, dynamite in a small package.

I once wrote about you when you were only 3 years old. As I watched you during that timeframe, I observed the way you interacted with this world, growing and learning—I learned from you. Even though you were but very small, deep within your little spirit grew a mighty oak. We are all created in different packaging but what is on the inside determines our destiny in this life. Your little size at "3" meant absolutely nothing to you, as you stepped out independently ready to conquer this ever-changing world. I watched you from a distance interact with others—stepping forth to challenges beyond a 3-year old capacity; however, the determination within you kept you treading forward and never retreating. You had a fighter mentality within that said, "I will not give up—I will not quit!" It is that strength within that will carry you far in this life. As that small seed within you continued to grow in beauty and strength, just like the mighty oak, you always remembered your roots. The mighty oak possesses all of its strength from deep within its root system. Your roots carry you all the way back to your Creator just like that of the oak. God has placed within you all that you are made of, and He will see you through every single storm in this life—throughout your days. Though the storms come and go, the mighty oak will sway back and forth. Many limbs may be weakened which fall or are removed, but the oak remains standing, as long as it is rooted deep within healthy soil. You too will face many storms in this life and these storms will remove from you those things that weaken you. Allow the trials in this life; remain connected to that which is healthy, and let go of those areas which will weaken you and bring you down.

Isaiah 61:3 (NLT) ³To all who mourn in Israel, he will give a crown of beauty for ashes, a joyous blessing instead of mourning, festive praise instead of despair. In their righteousness, they will be like great oaks that the LORD has planted for his own glory.

It is evident to see that God has given you a strong-will, but with that strong-will, you will have to endure many tests in this life in order that He molds you in the image of Jesus Christ. Remain righteous in the sight of the Lord, always—and He will create within you a perfect heart!

This book I dedicate to you this day, Charli—my "little oak tree" who has always loved to pray and in those sweet prayers of a child, they touched my life from the time you were very small. Your words—with every prayer were always filled with, "Let us have a good day." It was in those prayers that I began to think, what does that look like, which begins this book.

Table of Contents

Acknowledgement v

Dedication vii

Introduction xi

1 God's Ways and Thoughts........................1

2 The True Church....................................17

3 Wake Up America...................................29

4 God's Mercy & Great Love......................45

5 Trusting in a Good God in Your Storm......59

6 Rejoice, Today is a Good Day...................65

References 79

INTRODUCTION

As a writer, I normally have many books in the works—even if I am not sure what the outcome or the purpose of those books are at the time of thought. I say *"thought"* because being a Christian author, the Lord normally gives me a brief *"thought"* on a book and sometimes the title. However, like I said, I have many of those manuscripts in the works but can only compose one or two at one time. This particular book's *"thought"* was one that the Lord gave to me because of my granddaughter's prayers when she was just 3 years old. Today, Charli is 9 years old and still such a blessing to all that know her. When I first received the inspiration of this book, it was because she would always pray for every person to have a *"good day."*

One day, I asked her, *"Charli, what do you think a good day looks like?"* Before we dive into that question, I would like for every single person to ask themselves that same thing—what does a good day look like to those who claim to be Christians? Think about your answer before you continue.

The second thing I asked my granddaughter, *"What do you think a good day to the Lord looks like?"* Once again, ask yourself that same question. With your answers in mind, think about the world we live in today. I believe that the timing on the reflection to this book given to me by the Lord is one where our world, as we know it, has suddenly and strangely taken a turn where there is much confusion, tremendous fear, anxiety, and uncertainty. Yes—the coronavirus *(COVID-19)* has shaken the very foundations of the majority in this world today. It is during times like these, people begin to search for anything and everything to find answers and peace in a world that has somehow—almost overnight—changed and turned our very lives upside down. It is at times like these, people are desperate for some type of solace, but can solace be found?

I pray that everyone who reads this book does so with the expectation that they find something far greater—something that will turn our countries, nations—our world around for the better. I pray that we come together united as one people—changed societies, with motives to help those who are sick, the afflicted, the broken, the poor. *"Lord, I pray above all, that we have a good day—but, it is a good day for You, one that will open eyes to see and ears to hear—You will reign supreme over Your people, as they unite together as One."*

CHAPTER ONE
God's Ways and Thoughts

In the introduction, everyone should have answered the two questions. Before we begin to examine the answers to those two questions, we need to establish God's ways and His thoughts based on the Word of God not man's beliefs.

What we may think a good day looks like does not necessary mean that is what a good day looks like to God. Our answer to the first question will probably be quite different than the answer Biblically. Why? Because like the Scriptures tell us, God's ways and His thoughts are entirely different. Let's establish the way God thinks based Biblically.

In Isaiah 55, God said, *"For my thoughts are not your thoughts, neither are your ways my ways, declares the LORD."* I believe we have a hard time understanding these very words. Yes, we understand that we are NOT God, but do we really understand or even think about these words? I'm going to tell you, the Christian population today, many fail to realize the importance of those very words in Isaiah. If you were to stop and really think about what God may think a good day looks like, your answer would more than likely fall short unless you spent considerable time studying the Bible. However, today it is much easier to attend a church service, listen to someone give you a message, walk away with that message and just assume everything looks pretty good. The problem with this is that the majority of those who claim to be Christians fail to understand the Bible, seldom read the Bible, and probably never really study it—so, I believe it would be fair to say, most have no idea how God thinks or what His ways are and why.

I hate to teach out of context because far too often, the Word of God is taught that way. I will say that many times I touch on a particular Scripture without going back and explaining what was said in its entirety in those passages, but before I share any message, I have indeed studied the whole passage. Why am I saying this? Far too often, messages given today take a simple line of Scripture and teach what they believe it means without examining the full passage. It is quite alright to teach that one line, if you have already fully exhausted the whole passage—but, it falls on God's people to be wise—we are to take any teachings, mine included—where we go back and study the context as applied in the Word of God and examine it ourselves. Yet, how the Word is being taught from church to church differs and most do not take time to really challenge themselves on knowing Scripture. If we are not really studying ourselves to know the Word of God in truth, how could we possibly understand what a good day to God looks like? So again, our way of doing something is NOT His way which pertains to following His ways where we know His thoughts.

I'm not calling any names out particular because I have been in that very place where the majority of what I knew about the Bible came from teachings of man—and even though, I have always studied the Bible, I failed to realize that Scripture being taught out of context due to not examining the whole passage, many times is false. However, I came to a place where I wanted to know more and began to ask, seek, and knock—just like we are told to do in Scripture.

Let's begin to clarify what was being taught in Isaiah 55 prior to us being told that His ways and thoughts are not our ways and thoughts, and how detrimental this knowledge is to our not being led astray by false teachings. To clarify, if you begin reading these verses in 55, we are first taught about the compassion of the Lord—wow, it brings a chill to my whole body when I think about the Lord's compassion. Remember, His Words are life, their meanings are very advantageous—meanings that will either save you or lead you astray depending on where you are receiving your knowledge. Compassion should always bring chills knowing that none are worthy to even deserve His consideration of one day standing before Him as we are received into heaven. Here we are, not worthy by far—we are so incomplete—guilty, yes, we are all guilty—we are a frail people—we do not live up to ever being good enough to make it to heaven—we are nothing and He is everything, but yet, He loved us—and, He still loves us even though we have such shortcomings. Why? Why, would the God of the universe—the God who created each of us—the God who looks down on us in our triumphs, defeats, sins—why does He still love us? We are His creation, and He said it was good. *(Genesis 1:31)*

It is His great compassion for His creation that looks down upon man-kind and desires nothing more in the world than for His people to have eyes to see, ears to hear—that we choose to chase after Him. Yet, we spend countless hours, days, weeks, months, years chasing after this world that will one day—fade away! In Isaiah 55, in His compassion that He has for all of mankind, He pleads that we come, everyone—come if you thirst, if you have no money—come buy those things you need <u>without a price</u>. He is not talking about those things we need that cost money. He is talking about coming to Him—faith, trusting in Him—if you have needs, come to Him and He will fill you with all that you need. Yet—we spend our days working and buying—buying into this world, the world that will one day pass away—the world that does not care about you—you will live out your life *(hopefully)* and in the end, when you are facing your last days, what have you really gained? A name in this world? Perhaps, you have gained fame, fortune. Perhaps, you made an impact for the next generation. Or, perhaps you have not really spent your time wisely to gain anything. However, our only gain in this life that is meaningful, is how you lived pertaining to the Word of God. What you do in this life will determine where you spend eternity. Once more, what you do in this life may even determine how your children and grand-children spend eternity. Did you spend your time wisely or was it all about gaining the things in this world?

Let me say, it took me many years walking with the Lord where He began to enlighten my way of thinking to be able to understand what He wanted His people to know. It took me many years to know there was something far greater that can only be obtained through deep study of the Word of God that will radically change your life. It took me many years to comprehend the mind of Christ—His great compassion, His love, His wisdom, His knowledge, etc. Prior to walking in this myself, I looked at things just like the majority in the churches today. My downfall or rather lack of knowing truth—Biblical truth, was being absorbed in hours spent in what we call the church today. I was submerged into following a man's teachings rather than the Word of God. My thoughts lined up with all of those I associated with in the church circles, and my ways became their ways. Let me stress, I am by no means saying to anyone that we should not go to church. On the contrary, we are to be joined together with other believers—but, yes—it is extremely important that what we are being taught within the buildings we call church today, lines up with the Word of God. I have a whole section that will talk more about the modern-day churches today, but let me just establish, the Bible teaches that *"we"* are the church—those who claim to know Jesus Christ, that is. The church is NOT a building. We are to be joined together regardless if it is in a building, on the street, out in the desert, in the field—but, who is our teacher?

Who is our teacher? Who are we to learn from? This is a very important segment of knowledge—in knowing His ways and His thoughts, where we are not led astray. We are told Biblically, that we gain wisdom from the Lord and from His mouth come knowledge and understanding.

Proverbs 2:6 (ESV) For the LORD gives wisdom; from his mouth come knowledge and understanding.

This Scripture does not say that we gain wisdom, knowledge, or understanding from man. Again, it is the fear of the Lord that is the beginning of knowledge—but, fools despise wisdom and instruction.

Proverbs 1:7 (ESV) The fear of the LORD is the beginning of knowledge; fools despise wisdom and instruction.

I could go on and on with Scriptures that talk about knowledge, wisdom, and understanding—the Bible is full of those Scriptures, but I believe we all know that it is the Word of God that teaches us about wisdom and knowledge.

I have taught many times on these subjects and would like to briefly share something that I believe will give a clearer insight into how we apply the Bible. Gaining knowledge comes by studying. The root of the word is "know,"—we come to know about something by reading about it. When we were in school, there were many textbooks that we had to read and study in order to know what was being taught in that particular book. In order to pass tests on particular subjects, we had to gain the wisdom needed. The more you study—meaning the more you read, the more you know. Over time of reading and applying yourself to the subject at hand, the more wisdom you gain.

Let me make a point here—if you had a teacher that decided to teach you their version of history, where that teacher never gave you a text book—never had you read anything—the teacher merely taught you their own beliefs, what wisdom did you gain? The wisdom you gained was on someone else's beliefs instead of what was actually in the text book. You would grow up, go through life having gained wisdom based on a particular person and never really knowing if what that person taught was accurate or not. This pertains to every single person out there that teaches the Word of God—including myself. We are NOT told to gain our wisdom by man but rather by the Holy Spirit. Before I clarify that statement, let me conclude in saying, we gain knowledge first by what we read and study, which in turn leads to wisdom. Understanding only comes through time. Yes, as we actually walk through our lives based on the Bible—based on how we are told to walk as Christians which can only be done if the Holy Spirit is in your life—it will be actually learning how to walk through the storms of this life that gains the understanding. Briefly—an example is how you will walk through a storm such as the coronavirus! The world will mostly walk through this storm in fear, yet we are not to fear. Two Scriptures I want to share, yet there are many others—I believe these say much.

1 John 4:18 (ESV) There is no fear in love, but perfect love casts out fear. For fear has to do with punishment, and whoever fears has not been perfected in love.

What is love? God is love, there is no other love. It is not the love that the world knows, it is far greater. He is the definition of the word love. If you truly walk in Him, you will not fear. If you do fear, it is because His love has yet to be perfected in you. Now, I am not saying that fear will not come upon you—but, when it does, your walk with God will determine how you deal with that fear. Myself, when I find that I am allowing the fear to come, I have to get away from the world and alone with Him. It is at that place where I determine that whatever happens, it does not matter. If you truly belong to the Lord, your days are not promised. This life is merely a stepping stone to the life to come. Either you love this world or you love Him. If you love Him, your life is in His hands, and He already knows the number of your days.

Psalm 23:4 (ESV) Even though I walk through the valley of the shadow of death, I will fear no evil, for you are with me; your rod and your staff, they comfort me.

That Scripture sums it up. As a Christian, we should long for the day where we will stand before Him. If so, there should be no fear for He is with you.

To continue, as Christians—we are to be taught by the Holy Spirit, not man. Let me explain and give Scripture on what I mean. There are 3 places in the Bible where we are warned about the antichrist. In 1 John 2:18-27, John warns us about those who are false teachers among us. He tells us that they went out from us, but they were not of us. Meaning, there are those who walked among those that are true believers, but they were not of them. Yes, we are in these days. There are many today that claim to be followers of Jesus Christ, but it is evident by what they teach that they are leading others astray. Again, I will get into this further in another chapter. What I want to clarify, Paul goes on to say after speaking of those who do not know truth, that there is no need that anyone should teach us—if that same anointing abides in you as the first disciples, then it is that anointing—the Holy Spirit, that abides in you as one that belongs to Jesus Christ—His anointing, His Spirit, will teach you about everything that is true and is NOT a lie.

1 John 2:26-27(ESV)I write these things to you about those who are trying to deceive you. ²⁷But the anointing that you received from him abides in you, and you have no need that anyone should teach you. But as his anointing teaches you about everything, and is true, and is no lie—just as it has taught you, abide in him.

I'm not saying here that we are not to teach each other about the Bible, if I were saying that I would be a hypocrite myself because I am a Christian author and have written many books besides this one. What I am trying to establish is that we are to be taught by the Holy Spirit, so that false doctrine cannot lead us away from Jesus Christ. It is very simple—we are in those days, what days? The end days; if you do not believe that read the headlines, our world continues to escalate into darkness, trials, storms, tests, wickedness—yes, we are in a time that people who have never known the Lord are crying out to know Him. The main thing I am trying to emphasize here is that you cannot make it to heaven on someone else's relationship with God. We are told that there is no need that any man should teach us. Yes, there may be many who were led to the Lord from someone else's teachings, but once you are led in that direction, it is up to you to find Him truly! If you are not reading and studying Scripture on your own, there is a good chance that you are being led astray by false teachings. This is in the Bible three times because I believe it is important in this day and age. I will talk about this more in the next chapter, but we need to really understand that it takes each of us having that personal relationship with Jesus Christ to make it to heaven.

Again, in Hebrews where the new covenant was established in the New Testament versus the covenant in the Old Testament—

Hebrews 8:10-11(ESV) For this is the covenant that I will make with the house of Israel after those days, decided the Lord: I will put my law into their minds, and write them on their hearts, and I will be their God, and they shall be my people. ¹¹And they shall not teach, each one his neighbor and each one his brother, saying, 'Know the Lord,' for they shall all know me, from the least of them to the greatest.

In the Old Testament, also talking about the new covenant to be established in the New Testament it states—

Jeremiah 31:33-34(ESV) "For this is the covenant that I will make with the house of Israel after those days, declares the LORD: I will put my law within them, and I will write it on their hearts. And I will be their God, and they shall be my people. ³⁴And no longer shall each one teach his neighbor and each his brother, saying, 'Know the LORD,' for they shall all know me, from the least of them to the greatest, declares the LORD. For I will forgive their iniquity, and I will remember their sins no more."

I'm just going to throw a question out here that perhaps, you may not have thought about—prior to masses of Bibles being printed, how do you think that God's people remembered His Words? Yes, I know there were the writings that were read within the temples but let's look at our life today. We have no problem in America getting a Bible and most homes probably even own one. If we want to read something in the Bible, one can be easily obtained—and, if not, many can pull up any translation through google! What I am asking—in other countries, where they may not have access to Bibles, how do you think those who secretly meet as Christians know His Words? I don't think any of us can memorize the whole Bible. I have seen pastors who work hard at doing so, but it is not necessary. Why? If you live out your life as a Christian, really loving the Lord and spending time studying His Word—daily—weekly, when you need a Scripture, it comes to your mind at the time you need it because the same Spirit that lived in Jesus Christ lives in those who strive to walk with the Lord. It has always amazed me that anytime I have shared in the streets, women's retreats, with someone that the Lord just led across my path—the Scriptures would rise up within me and come out of my mouth. Why? Because I spent hours in His Word; I poured into Him and He poured into me. He said He would never leave nor forsake us. I could go on and on, but I have come to trust that He is always there with me just when I need Him. His Word is always there with me just when I need it—His Word is powerful; His Word heals the sick, sets the captive free, delivers those from oppression, comforts, brings peace that passes all understanding, etc.

However, what about those who have not had access to the Word of God? What about during the days there were NOT Bibles? I'm telling you, if the same Spirit that raised Jesus Christ from the dead lives in you, His Words will be in you when you need them. There have also been times in my life when I was giving a message and words would pour out of me that I had not heard. At these times, my mind would be thinking, *"Is this in the Bible?"* Afterwards, thanks to google, I would search to see if what I said was in the Bible—there it was because He said that the same Spirit dwells in those who walk with Him. This is powerful stuff—He is powerful—He is the same today as He was yesterday. He has not changed—but what we call the church today has changed!

Deuteronomy 4:2 (ESV) You shall not add to the word that I command you, nor take from it, that you may keep the commandments of the LORD your God that I command you.

Deuteronomy 12:32 (ESV) "Everything that I command you, you shall be careful to do. You shall not add to it or take from it."

Revelation 22:18-19 (ESV) I warn everyone who hears the words of the prophecy of this book: if anyone adds to them, God will add to him the plagues described in this book, [19]and if anyone takes away from the words of the book of this prophecy, God will take away his share in the tree of life and in the holy city, which are described in this book.

We are promised that same Spirit that dwelt in Jesus Christ to those who believe.

John 14:15-17(ESV) "If you love me, you will keep my commandments. [16]And I will ask the Father, and he will give you another Helper, to be with you forever, [17]even the Spirit of truth, whom the world cannot receive, because it neither sees him nor knows him. You know him, for he dwells with you and will be in you.

This is the Holy Spirit, the Comforter, the one that Jesus promised would be with us when He went to His Father. Jesus goes on to tell us in John, that it is the Holy Spirit that will teach us.

John 14:25-26 (ESV) "These things I have spoken to you while I am still with you. [26]But the Helper, the Holy Spirit, whom the Father will send in my name, he will teach you all things and bring to your remembrance all that I have said to you.

I needed to establish this to help those understand when we follow a particular denomination, movement, man, woman—the dangers are that you are basing your Christianity off of someone else's opinion. I'm not saying that all opinions out there are wrong, but we must know we are following God's ways and understanding His thoughts. We are warned three times because it is important—so important that it is a life or death situation. If whoever you are listening to instead of the Holy Spirit, you are basing your *"after this world"* life on words of a mere man or woman, this can be extremely dangerous. It is Russian roulette—you are playing with your own life. Let me also emphasize this, many may say that God shows them that the person they are listening to is from Him—please don't be deceived. I have heard this many times—if you never spend time in the Word of God, you are treading in dangerous waters. There are many voices out there to deceive you. We can only truly come to know our Lord and Savior through His Word. He tells us to ask, seek, and knock. It is asking Him, seeking Him, knocking for Him. There is no place in Scripture that teaches you to ask, seek, and knock to a person who claims to be a Christian. To know Him is to know His Word, only! Jesus was in the beginning because He was the Word, and He was made flesh and dwelt among us. *(John 1:18)*

Let's just assume you were adopted, and you grew up to be a young man or woman. During the years you grew up there was no one to tell you about your father because no one even knew who he was. So, you decided to try and find him. You finally came to a place where you found out that he was no longer living, but someone gave you a book that belonged to him where he wrote about his life. You brought it home but never picked it up to read it. Over the years, you met different people who said, *"Yes, I met your dad before—,"* or *"Oh, I remember Him—."* So, now you have accumulated an idea of who you think your father was based on your knowledge gained by men along the way you met. So, you live out your life doing things your way while thinking, *"It's all good because my dad was okay with this. Yes, I can do that because my dad did the same thing."* I think you know where I am going with this, but let's get to the end of this story. The day comes when you finally die and, in the darkness, you are led to a light. Standing in that light, you see the man who was your father. He takes one look at you and says, *"Depart from me, for I never knew you—,"* you are shocked, *"But, no—I'm your son, I was told that I was your son—father, do you not remember how I acknowledged you to many—I even gave money for your cause—there were even others that followed me in supporting your people—,"* but He once again says, *"Depart from me, for I never knew you—."*

No, I am not against the church at all—I am not against those who are teaching the true gospel—but, I am against those who are not stressing the importance of knowing Jesus Christ personally.

You see, our ways are not his ways because the majority want to follow the majority. If it looks good, it must be God. We think that way—we always want the biggest, the best, the most vibrant. I can remember stepping out from the *"big"* church to attend the *"small"* church. My first thoughts were, *"Lord, where is the coffee shop; where is the children's ministry; where is the elaborate bands, technology, etc. to entertain me."* We look for the best because that is the way we think, but what if the best is small? What if the best does not have the vibrant music? What if the best has a very small children's church? I found myself having to question everything when God spoke to me and said, *"Are you here to learn of me or for the entertainment?"* Again, when I walked away from *"the big church"* to spend time alone with God for 6 months, I felt as though I had lost everything, when he asked me, *"If you do lose everything and all you have is me, is that not enough?"*

I believe we have to ask ourselves those questions, or at least, we have to ask, *"Do we really want to know Jesus Christ or are we just looking for a place to have a social life?"* We are told in the Word of God that only the few even find the narrow road that leads to heaven, but yet most want to follow the crowds. I was there; I know. We think more is better, but maybe God thinks less is better. If there are 100 people that believe something to be true and only 2 that disagree, we will tend to side with the 100, why? Because we think the majority must be right—yet, the Bible clearly tells us that the majority will never see heaven. I'm telling you, that these are things to consider. In Haggai 1, the Word of the Lord said to consider your ways. The Scriptures in Haggai are talking about sowing much but harvesting little, eating but never having enough, drinking but never having your fill, clothing yourself but never being warm, earning wages and putting them into a bag with holes. Yes, it is speaking of our ways—we always want more of this world, never satisfied with what we have. Yes, the time is now to consider our ways—our ways are not His ways. Our thoughts are not His thoughts.

CHAPTER TWO
The True Church

I will try to briefly examine two items in this chapter. Speaking of the true church, there are far too many Scriptures which clarify what the true church looks like, as well as the many Scriptures on those teaching falsely in the day and time we are living. I have taught on both of these subjects many times and have elaborated extensively in previous books. Therefore, for this book I will try to just touch on a few items and make it as brief as possible.

To begin with, we are told in Scripture—in the last days there will be many rise up to lead others astray.

Matthew 24:4-5(ESV) And Jesus answered them, "See that no one leads you astray. ⁵For many will come in my name, saying, 'I am the Christ,' and they will lead many astray."

For more clarity, Jesus also spoke of false prophets in sheep's clothing.

Matthew 7:15 (ESV) "Beware of false prophets, who come to you in sheep's clothing but inwardly are ravenous wolves."

We also know according to Scripture that the gate is wide and the way easy that leads to destruction, while the gate is narrow that leads to life is hard and only few even find it.

Matthew 7:13(ESV) "Enter by the narrow gate. For the gate is wide and the way is easy that leads to destruction, and those who enter by it are many. ¹⁴For the gate is narrow and the way is hard that leads to life, and those who find it are few.

A few quick points to make—
- Evidently, most Christians believe they would recognize a wolf, even though Jesus says otherwise. Where does He say this? First, a warning of wolves; second, stating that only the few find the way that leads to life.
- Among the Christian community, all seem to believe they will make it to heaven, even though this is not Biblical. Again, we are told that only the few find the way that leads to life.

To emphasize my points, Jesus felt that He needed to warn those who desired to follow Him. His warning was on wolves in sheep-clothing. What was He saying— there would be those out there that looked like a sheep, sounded like a sheep—everything about them seemed to portray the image of a sheep. This is what He meant because this is what He said. WARNING- they are wolves, but you will not be able to determine this because everything about them is going to look like a sheep.

I have said this many times to those I have ministered to and in books, Jesus was not talking about those such as: Charles Manson, Jim Jones, Warren Jeffs, and many more. Yes, these were cults that oppressed and controlled those following, but these were far less dangerous than the wolves in sheep clothing. The cults above, their followers were nothing compared to what we see within the churches that are led by wolves. You see, Charles Manson did not look like a sheep.

Charles Manson to the majority looked evil and he was. His followers were those who were weak and looking for someone to lead them. However, Jesus warned of the wolves in sheep clothing because they are the most dangerous of all. These men and women, look like a sheep in all aspects—this is why we are warned. It is in those days, the days we are living in that the false prophets will be the many and they will lead the many away as those following them believe that they hear from God.

There are several issues with this. I will not discuss all of them, again—these are topics that I go deep into in other books that are printed. I just briefly want to share where we are today—where we are during COVID-19 and why. So, to continue, these churches are the ones that give the people what they want to hear instead of what they need to hear.

2 Timothy 4:3 (ESV) For the time is coming when people will not endure sound teaching, but having itching ears they will accumulate for themselves teachers to suit their own passions.

People follow their teachings because it sounds good. They have followers because people want to feel like they are involved in something great. They want to feel that they are doing something for the Lord. I'm not saying it is not good to feel that you are being used by God, but if you are following what is false and you are being infiltrated with their messages that do not line up with the Word of God, where does this lead you in the end? Will you be one that is welcomed into Heaven or one that is turned away? Remember, Jesus was speaking to those who considered themselves to be

Christians when He turned away the many and said, *"Depart from me for I never knew you."*

The problem with the teachings in these man-made churches is that they never really share how a person is really saved. Yes, they quote different Scriptures and have people say their little tag lines and such, but there is only one way to get to Heaven—a one-on-one individual relationship with Jesus Christ. You will never gain Heaven when you never seek Him. You will never gain Heaven if you do not hear that small inner voice that speaks to you. I say this so often and will once again, it is your own personal relationship with Jesus Christ that insures your salvation. If you never read and study His Word, you do not know Him. I have already shared this in chapter one, but it takes those who really and truly love Him that will seek Him. You seek to find and you find by spending time in His Word alone!

2 John 2:3 (ESV) Everyone who goes on ahead and does not abide in the teaching of Christ, does not have God. Whoever abides in the teaching has both the Father and the Son.

This is abiding in His Word. This is not abiding in the words that have been taught to you by a man or a woman or even by me. You do not have the Father nor the Son when you never seek for Him. Remember, as children we would play *"hide and seek,"* and in doing so, the idea was to keep seeking until you find. The great news is that our Father does not really hide from us because He desires that we find Him. We must continue to seek until we find; you will not get to Heaven on someone else's shirttail.

1 John 2:3 (ESV) And by this we know that we have come to know him, if we keep his commandments.

Again, if you are following His commandments based off of what a man has taught you—beware, it may be accurate but it can never be completely accurate if you are not following Him yourself. It is about you hearing from Him and then about you following Him in what He has planned for your life, not someone else's.

1 John 4:6 (ESV) We are from God. Whoever knows God listens to us; whoever is not from God does not listen to us. By this we know the Spirit of truth and the spirit of error.

I want to touch on a few things with this Scripture in 1 John spoken by the Apostle John and the Scripture below that Paul spoke in 1 Corinthians.

1 Corinthians 11:1-2 (ESV) Be imitators of me, as I am of Christ. ²Now I commend you because you remember me in everything and maintain the traditions even as I delivered them to you.

John and Paul were both disciples of Jesus Christ. Jesus' disciples gave up all to follow Him. All of them left all to follow and do the works that Jesus called them to do. They all suffered and they all died for Him. I remember years ago, a pastor saying to his congregation, *"Follow me as I follow Christ."* I can remember my thoughts and how I cringed when he spoke those words. He said that if Paul could say that, we should also be able to say that. The problem I have with this is that I have yet to see anyone that sacrificed and did what the disciples in the Bible did. To take this a bit farther, in America, I have not seen many pastors or people who claim to be Christians that have given up much of their life for the sake of the gospel. In 1 John, John was merely saying that those who listened to them knew God and those who did not, did not know Him. Yes, we are to teach and preach the Word of God to all who He sends across our path, but in those teachings, we must assure people that they cannot get to Heaven by just listening to what we teach. Our purpose is to lead them to the Word of God in order that they find truth—the real truth!

What is true and what is false? That is easy—truth is the Word of God and everything in it. We can gather together with other believers, but we always run back to our Father. We always seek Him that we are filled with His presence, that we are filled with His Spirit. Like I taught in chapter one, we are to be taught by the Holy Spirit. We should be in communication with His Spirit. If we never seek Him, we will never find Him and the Spirit will not live within us.

John 8:44 (ESV) You are of your father the devil, and your will is to do your father's desires. He was a murderer from the beginning, and has nothing to do with the truth, because there is no truth in him. When he lies, he speaks out of his own character, for he is a liar and the father of lies.

I know this is harsh, but let's face it—if those who are teaching you are doing so falsely, there is no truth in them. What desires are you following in this life? Are your desires for those things in this world or for those things of God? That one is pretty cut and dry, but it is very true. The disciples of yesterday, their desires were to continually be in communion with the Father in order that they were doing the will of the Father. Whose will are you following today? Do you even know what God's will is for your life? He did not create those who are His to spend all the days of their life pouring into the things of this world. He did not create those who are His to fill their desires with this world. Ask yourself this question, is your heaven on this earth or is your Heaven for your life after death?

James 4:4 (ESV) You adulterous people! Do you not know that friendship with the world is enmity with God? Therefore whoever wishes to be a friend of the world makes himself an enemy of God.

We cannot be a friend with the world if we want to be a friend with God. Again, this is our choice of who we are following—a man-made ministry or the true church of Jesus Christ. Far too often, we compromise in what we are called to do, knowing if we really stand up for true Christianity, we will lose friends. We also compromise by trying to fit in with the crowds where we have many friends. It comes down to, who are you living for? Is this life your heaven or the next life?

I'm really going to step on toes right now, but I hope that we all have our big boy and big girl pants on where we can rightfully judge our own actions—because this is between you and God. Today, with all the new technology, it is easy to see why you cannot tell the Christians from the non-Christians. Playing church is by no means attractive to God. If you spend much time outside of what we call church today, you will find many that do not frequent a building labeled *"church"* because they do not teach about the God known in the streets. *(Again-I am not referring to all churches today)*

Todays Christians, the many *(majority)*—are no different than the world. They buy up the latest technologies, phones, computers, gaming systems—they go to work, come home, perhaps attend church services, many different scenarios—but, they spend very little time and many spend no time developing that relationship with Jesus Christ.

Yes, here we are—2020, COVID-19 rampant in all nations. Fear coming from every angle—how many people would dare say, this is a good day? In Isaiah 55 that we touched on in chapter one, God also tells us to incline our ears and come to Him to hear. He is always trying to get our attention. He tells us to seek Him while He may be found—this is drastic measures and we are in drastic times. We are to call upon Him while He is near—He may not always be near. He pleads to those who are wicked, yes—God loves the wicked. He also pleads to the unrighteous man to return to the Lord, why? Those who call upon Him, those who seek Him, He will have compassion on them. It is after all of this, He tells us that the way we think, it's wrong—it's not the way He thinks. Our thoughts, their wrong—it's not His thoughts. The things we do, are not pleasing to God because it is not His ways. We have our own ways. We don't wake up every morning and pray, *"Lord show me what you want me to do this day."* Perhaps some do this, but the majority do not have time for this. I have heard people say many times, *"I don't have time to pray—I don't have time to read the Bible,"* but yet, we have time to do those things that we truly desire. God is always taking back seat. Well, here we are in a crisis—what's it going to take? Will His people turn back to Him? That's doubtful, they may have for a short time after 911, but it didn't last. They may have after Hurricane Katrina, but it didn't last.

We have to understand that the masses in the churches today are not the few—they are the many and it is only the few that make it to Heaven.

Matthew 7:13-14, 21-23 (ESV) [13]"Enter by the narrow gate. For the gate is wide and the way is easy that leads to destruction, and those who enter by it are many. [14]For the gate is narrow and the way is hard that leads to life, and those who find it are few. [21]"Not everyone who says to me, 'Lord, Lord,' will enter the kingdom of heaven, but the one who does the will of my Father who is in heaven. [22]On that day many will say to me, 'Lord, Lord, did we not prophesy in your name, and cast out demons in your name, and do many mighty works in your name?' [23]And then will I declare to them, 'I never knew you; depart from me, you workers of lawlessness.'

We are told that only few make it to Heaven, why is this? It's because we have gotten comfortable going to the man-made churches and allowing a man or woman to give us their interpretation of what Christianity looks like. The problem with this is you cannot be saved that way. Salvation is a relationship with Jesus Christ; it is not a magic formula where you recite a few lines and presto—you are part of the family. Look at the stories in the Bible of how they were saved; look at the stories in the Bible to know what a church really looks like. We can learn so much if we would just study the Word of God.

A relationship, like any relationship, is where time is invested with another person. A man and a woman do not get married and spend years never speaking to each other. If they did, I would dare say there was no relationship. You cannot know someone when you never communicate. The problem is that most people are living like the world and they have those things they are passionate about, such as video games, clothing, shoes, sports—these take up everything on the inside of them where there is no room for God.

I sat in a church service one time where there was a survey done, so to speak, and I'm going to say about 95% of the people who claimed to be Christians had never heard God speak. It really terrified me because if you have never heard Him speak to you, you cannot possibly be saved. We do not stand before Jesus Christ one day where He says, *"Oh, you are Baptist—your door to heaven is right there. I see you are Catholic—yes, your door is over there to heaven. Non-denomination, ah yes, the large door over there will lead you to heaven. Let's see, the prosperity-gospel folks—well, we created a special door for all of you, it looks just like a large jet."*

Not to be facetious, but sometimes I am just amazed by what others say. It is evident that the majority seldom even read the Bible, and well, statistics show the numbers to be far greater that do not read nor study the Word of God. It is no wonder that the Bible is so misrepresented based on the numerous doctrines that teach their own philosophies. I am not against organizations so prevalent coming together to share Jesus, but I am against those that look nothing like the Bible, as many have begun to emerge to look like the world. I can only speak these things in hopes that my purpose is fulfilled where each of us questions our relationship with Jesus Christ. I by no means can change anyone nor make them seek Jesus; however, I can be used to at least bring up these subjects in hopes that there may be some who choose to seek Jesus to a deeper degree where they find and develop that true relationship.

CHAPTER THREE
Wake Up America

I want to talk about America. This can pertain to every place in the world but being an American, I need to address our country—our ways—our thoughts!

I live in Louisiana, and I remember the exact day that 911 happened. The timeframe was just a little over one year from my daughter's death. I was still in turmoil from my own loss and the pain of all those who died overwhelmed my emotions, as it did our whole nation. America being hit on our own soil? America, the greatest and strongest country ever. America, home of the brave—America, home of the free—America, a land with plenty, a land with opportunity, a land where the American dream is possible, a land where you can be educated, a land where you can reach far and wide for many a dream to be achieved. I am afraid that day will always be remembered as an awakening that pride cometh before a fall.

Proverbs 16:18-19 (ESV) Pride goes before destruction, and a haughty spirit before a fall. ^{19}It is better to be of a lowly spirit with the poor than to divide the spoil with the proud.

America is prideful. The word haughty means arrogant and superior. Yes. America has been proud to the point that we have always believed ourselves superior. After all, we were the land of the free—the land of the brave—the land where dreams could come true—the land of plenty. Let's face it, no one thought that America could have ever been attacked on our own soil. Yet, we were! It reminds me of the Titanic. It was the most glorious ship ever built for that time. They never believed that the Titanic could be sunk, but we know what happened. At what cost did the pride of those who built the Titanic and those who believed it could never sink—at what cost did they pay? Many died that day because of pride. Now, I am not saying that it was the pride that caused the Titanic to sink, but the Bible does tell us that pride cometh before a fall. Do many innocent people die because of pride? Well, unfortunately, they do.

Let's not look at America as a whole, let's look at every single person today who lives in America. We are all guilty—we are all to blame. At what cost does our own selfish pride cause those very things we depend on to fall? At what cost does our selfishness cause our lives and those around us to fall? I say selfishness because most are busy about their own lives—getting ahead in this world—striving to gain more wealth—spending years to gain the necessary education to succeed in this world, while what we call the church today has gone to hell. I know that is strong language but bear with me. Jesus gave us an example of being humble, if you study the gospels. Jesus rode into Jerusalem on a colt or a foal. *(Mark 11)* The significance of his entry into Jerusalem comes from Zechariah.

Zechariah 9:9 (ESV) Rejoice greatly, O daughter of Zion! Shout aloud, O daughter of Jerusalem! Behold, your king is coming to you; righteous and having salvation is he, humble and mounted on a donkey, on a colt, the foal of a donkey.

I remember hearing a preacher, as he was sharing with his followers—manipulating rather, how God had spoken to him to buy a new jet to add to his collection, yes—one of those prosperity gospel preachers. He only needed $54 million; I believe that was the number. He made the remark, that if Jesus was to come back today, He wouldn't do it on a colt, He would come back by jet. I have to say, I am amazed at what people listen to out there—but, then I shouldn't be amazed because the majority do not read or study the Bible. First, the preacher who said this was arrogant or rather prideful with his remark because he is not God, and he cannot claim what God would do or how he would go about doing it. Second, if the pastor knew anything about the Bible, he would know that Jesus did not ride on the colt because He couldn't have had something far greater, if that was the way it was supposed to be—Jesus chose the colt to be humble because He is our example. And, what happens to those who are prideful? What happens according to the Word of God? Pride comes before a fall.

Let me say, most look at the American churches today based on their numbers. However, God said that His ways are not ours and His thoughts are not ours. Thank goodness for that, but the problem is that people do not study the Word of God themselves, so they have no idea if what they are listening to even lines up with the Word of God. People are following what looks good, what feels good, what entertains them, etc. People would rather make it to heaven by jet instead of by a horse. The sad truth is that your jet is not going to get you to heaven. We want to follow that glorious church that looks good on the outside—the outer perimeter of anything, that which is tangible. That which looks good that we can see with our eyes to include the buildings, landscapes, furnishings, etc. These are all outer perimeters. Yet, the Bible tells us to not judge a person by what they see on the outside but what is on the inside. So, what does that mean exactly? Remember again, the way God thinks is not the way we think. When we see a person commit sin, we automatically think that they are not right with God—yet, all of the disciples sinned at one point and David is our best example on one who sinned. Yet, David was a man after God's own heart. We do not judge someone by their actions because we do not know if they are running back to God ashamed of that sin and looking for strength through Him to overcome.

What is on the inside of someone, that is where we are to judge. Many of these large mega-churches are out there pouring money into works, but do not let that fool you—those that lead these churches are glorifying in their own wealth and riches. Remember, works alone will not save you. We are told Biblically not to look on the outside but to look on the inside of a person. This is two-fold, there are many out there who are judged by their outward works but inwardly, they are ravenous wolves.

Matthew 7:15 (ESV) "Beware of false prophets, who come to you in sheep's clothing but inwardly are ravenous wolves."

On another note, many out there are judged outwardly by their sins, yet—they could very well be as David, running to God instead of from Him. These may possibly realize that they need a savior and are constantly crying out to God to redeem them. In our world, we judge both of these wrongly because our ways and thoughts are not His ways and thoughts. The one who does good works to be seen by man, on the inside could be as far from God as anyone could possibly be. A question to be asked in these cases, what are their motives and do those motives line up with the Word of God? Motives—are their motives to be praised by man? Are their motives to gain the riches of this world? Are their motives to gain a place in this world, acceptance, fame, fortune, wealth, etc.? Are they loved by this world and are they a friend of this world? We should then go back and examine their lives to see if they line up with the lives of the disciples in Biblical days. It does not take much examining to be able to determine the wolves from the true followers of Jesus Christ.

And again, the ones we judge by their sins we see on the outside, we consider those as not being right with God. Yet—those could actually be closer to God than all those who are perceived on the outside to be righteous. These are strange thoughts but thoughts, indeed. Our ways and thoughts are not His.

1 Samuel 16:7 (ESV) But the LORD said to Samuel, "Do not look on his appearance or on the height of his stature, because I have rejected him. For the LORD sees not as man sees: man looks on the outward appearance, but the LORD looks on the heart."

Paul, in 1 Corinthians 5, is talking about the condition of the church, when he says—

1 Corinthians 5:12-13 (ESV) For what have I to do with judging outsiders? Is it not those inside the church whom you are to judge? ¹³God judges those outside. Purge the evil person from among you.

These are powerful words spoken, but they are so true. The only way any of us are saved is by what is on the inside of us. What did David look like on the outside? He looked like a sinner—no one witnessed David running back and forth crying out to God. David was not trying to be seen by man; He desired God. So, we may look like David on the outside living in our sin, but if we are turning to Jesus Christ time and time again, He is still doing a work in us—just as He did in David. Why is this? It is because we are in communion with God. I told someone one time, *"If you see me do this, just know that you don't have to say anything because God is still dealing with me on it, and I always go back to make it right."* You see, if you are right with God, He will not leave you alone when you do something wrong. He will keep on until you make it right. Sometimes it takes many, many times to change a bad habit—but, those bad habits never change when there is no real communication with God. We might can overcome them for a time, but we will also fall back into the same sins if we are not walking close to the Lord.

You see, our way of thinking is that we judge others by their good deeds. We judge the churches today by their good deeds, so much so, that we all want to be a part of such marvelous wealthy congregations in order to put our money into the good works that will never lead anyone to heaven.

Ephesians 2:8-9 (ESV) For by grace you have been saved through faith. And this is not your own doing. It is the gift of God, ⁹not a result of works, so that no one may boast.

I am not saying that good works are a bad thing, but what I am saying is that we are to judge by what we see inwardly not on the outside.

Matthew 23:25-28 (ESV) "Woe to you, scribes and Pharisees, hypocrites! For you clean the outside of the cup and the plate, but inside they are full of greed and self-indulgence. 26You blind Pharisee! First clean the inside of the cup and the plate, that the outside also may be clean. 27Woe to you, scribes and Pharisees, hypocrites! For you are like whitewashed tombs, which outwardly appear beautiful, but within are full of dead people's bones and all uncleanness. 28So you also outwardly appear righteous to others, but within you are full of hypocrisy and lawlessness."

When I see a mega-pastor pleading for more money to buy him another jet, I immediately look to see what is in his heart. Looking on the inside is rightly judged according to the Word of God. On the inside, I first saw where he twisted the Scriptures to fit his gain which is deceit. I then look at what the Bible says which again, does not paint a picture of a man of God nor a sheep—but rather a wolf in sheep clothing. We are not living in the days of great prosperity among God's people—no, we are living in the days of the church. Spurgeon said it best when he noted that the Old Testament promise was one of prosperity but the New Testament promise is one of tribulation.[1] Far too often, pastors use the Scriptures in the old testament to gain their wealth. We are the church, and we are the ones to prepare for the second coming of Jesus Christ. His disciples while He walked this earth, none of them gained riches. Jesus was their example of a Godly man being humble and He is our example, as well. All of the first disciples lost everything for the gospel's sake. They were all humbled. Their motives were for lost souls not for riches. If people would study the gospels, it is a clear picture of how to be humble. It is a clear picture of how to live as a true believer in Jesus Christ because it is about saving the lost and gaining heaven. These prosperity preachers have lost that. To them it is about gaining the world and not heaven. To them this world is their paradise, as they strive to gain more and more. It is about laying up treasures on earth not in heaven. You cannot have both—either, one you will love and the other you will hate.

Matthew 6:19-21 (ESV) "Do not lay up for yourselves treasures on earth, where moth and rust destroy and where thieves break in and steal, ^{20}but lay up for yourselves treasures in heaven, where neither moth nor rust destroys and where thieves do not break in and steal. ^{21}For where your treasure is, there your heart will be also.

Prior to the Scripture above, it makes note of those who outwardly do good deeds to be seen by man.

Matthew 6:1 (ESV) "Beware of practicing your righteousness before other people in order to be seen by them, for then you will have no reward from your Father who is in heaven.

If you desire this world, to be seen as righteous among man, to be seen on the outside as good among those in this world, this will be your heaven. If your desire for this world outweighs your desire for heaven, you will forfeit heaven. However, if you desire heaven to a degree that you are willing to lose everything, you will gain heaven. Do you understand why the majority want to attend church where the masses are? They want to live for this world, most have no desire to live for the world to come. They enjoy the riches and wealth of this world, not spending their time and money on helping others and saving the world.

This brings me back to pride. We are a prideful nation because America became great. It was alright for America to become a great nation, but remember, it was supposed to be—One Nation Under God! What happened? With anything, as sinners, we gain and we only want more—never being satisfied. Everyone has been guilty of this—and, we become prideful.

America is so very prideful. America thinks of herself as being the greatest country. Perhaps, we have looked to be the greatest country because of our freedoms—yet, it is a very dangerous thing when we fail to be humble for all those things that God has blessed us with. When we gain wealth or anything of greatness at an alarming rate, those things seem to change who we are from the inside out. Having the best of everything is not always a blessing. In fact, having more is not always better than having less. If we are to look at the faith issue, when you always have more, why would you need faith? When would you ever need to exercise your faith?

Yes, when 911 impacted the United States, America was humbled. But—what happened afterwards? Afterwards, our leaders stood up prideful and declared that America would rebuild, America would be great again! Pride cometh before a fall. When faced with any tragedy, the last thing we need to do is become prideful. In any circumstance, we need to get down on our hands and knees and repent for our pride and beg God to not turn away from this nation—One Nation, that was built under God! A new beginning comes down to God leading and us following humbly. I can tell you that our laws today continue to walk so far away from God—it will take a people demanding that God be put back into the schools, back into government, back into marriage and the laws of marriage! Yes, we need a revival but that will never come as long as our country is divided among what is righteous and what is evil.

Next, Hurricane Katrina hit New Orleans which shattered our nation once again as multitudes from other states and our government came to help us rebuild. Katrina hit in 2005 and since then, we have rebuilt. People were scattered all over the United States, some returning and some never came back. I could go on and on about destruction with many hurricanes, fires that have ravaged our nation and many other countries—earthquakes, tsunamis, and on and on. I am sure everyone could tell of other catastrophes, but where is God in all of this?

God is right here in the middle of all of this. God has allowed every single thing to happen because He is God, and He is a jealous God. Yes, we need to wake up America. God gave us this country, founded on Godly principles but gradually, we are pushing God out of this country. We have removed Him from our schools, we continually try to strip Him from our government—YES, He used to be in politics—yes, He did! Thanks to our current president, President Trump, who has stood up to the people proclaiming Jesus Christ! But—due to our division among this country on the choice of who our president is, once again it is pride that comes before a fall.

Let me stir up a few thousand people here. Did you know that the Bible tells us that no one—NO ONE—is in a place of governing authority except from God—He instituted those to be there.

Romans 13:1 (ESV) Let every person be subject to the governing authorities. For there is no authority except from God, and those that exist have been instituted by God.

We are to pray for those in authority; we are to respect their leadership, even if we do not agree with them.

1 Timothy 2:1-2 (ESV) First of all, then, I urge that supplications, prayers, intercessions, and thanksgivings be made for all people, ²for kings and all who are in high positions, that we may lead a peaceful and quiet life, godly and dignified in every way.

When we act in defiance of what we should do, when we stand up to God and refuse to agree with His Word, no wonder we do not have peace in our lives today—no wonder our lives are filled with stresses of this world—no wonder our world as we know it today is in turmoil. In 1 Timothy, it clearly states that we do these things in order to have a peaceful life. Wow-is your COVID-19 working for you today? Do we claim to be a Christian yet slander our president? Would we dare NOT pray for him because we do not agree with him? If you are not in agreement, it is God that you are wrestling with. Let's see how that works for you if COVID-19 hits your home and your family. If you have no peace, perhaps it is time for you to get down on your hands and knees and repent to the only true God for mercy and forgiveness in your life. Yes, my words are very offensive at times, but did you know that the Bible is the most offensive book ever written? Perhaps, you did not know that because your knowledge of the Bible comes solely from a man or woman who claim they are right with God. Here we go again—honor the emperor!

1 Peter 2:17 (ESV)Honor everyone. Love the brotherhood. Fear God. Honor the emperor.

No, we do not have an emperor in this country, but let's get real—we are to honor those in authority, He placed all in those high positions. Do we fear God today? No, we are prideful—we are arrogant—we act as though we do not need God and never cry out for Him until we are faced with circumstances beyond our control. What now America? What now? We want to cry out to a God to fix our lives today. We want a God to transform lives back to pre-COVID-19, but are we willing to do what God requires?

2 Chronicles 7:14 (ESV) if my people who are called by my name humble themselves, and pray and seek my face and turn from their wicked ways, then I will hear from heaven and will forgive their sin and heal their land.

It has taken years for America to gradually push God out of our lives. We, a proud nation, decided that we no longer needed Him in politics. Even while COVID-19 is going on, I have seen Facebook remarks of those running down our government, the president—blaming him for the disease, as it is. I truly hope those doing so are not claiming to be Christians, for if they are, I am truly ashamed that in one breath you have those claiming to be a Christian and the other breath they are crucifying President Trump. Here we are, a nation that wants to claim to be a Christian nation, but yet, it is on our own terms, right? Yes, it's okay to go to church; it's okay to claim to be a Christian, but forbid that we allow Him in politics—forbid that we allow Him back in our schools—forbid that we do away with laws that have gone on the books that defile the Bible. If you are constantly in disarray over our government, your god may not be the God of the Bible, not if you only turn to Him when it benefits your own selfish lives. The true God has gradually been replaced in our society, as Hollywood sets the standard for what is right and what is not—and the largest culprit of all that are leading the majority astray comes from the so-called churches that have gained popularity with this world.

Yes, the churches today are in a sad shape when we have pastors that do not even know the Word of God. We have these massive churches that tickle the ears of the multitudes in order to fill their congregations giving people what they want in a church instead of what the Bible proclaims a true church is. In politics, we have the masses, even those who claim to be Christians, that will vote for women's rights to have abortions—shame on you! A baby is life and we are NOT God—Christians do NOT vote to bring those into office that will willingly push in agendas that kill the unborn. Above all, God has been removed from most homes, as they have become secular. They may claim to be Christians, but their lifestyles show nothing of true Christianity. Their lifestyles are no different than the world, as they fill their lives with the same entertainment, spend countless hours surfing the web, glued to their cell phones/text messaging, and the massive entertainment from movies, gaming, etc. for hours on end. Am I surprised that the coronavirus or

COVID-19 has infiltrated our world? I am not surprised in the least. God is an angry God, yes—He is! I am thankful that He is because I would rather go through something like COVID-19, where I have the opportunity to check my own life and get it right before I die and do not make heaven.

Get real people, EVERYONE DOES NOT MAKE IT TO HEAVEN, THAT IS BIBLICAL! We go to funerals and they are all done the same way, giving the families assurance that their loved ones are in heaven. We are NOT God and we do not know this! We live day in and day out never even thinking about God because we are too busy trying to keep up with having all the latest gadgets, the newest I-phones, computers, etc. We spend countless hours in front of the television streaming any and everything we can because we desire this world and all it has to offer. None are worthy of Him, and woah to those who choose this world over God. He desires that His people will turn back to Him and the great news is that some of them will because of the COVID-19! Yes, many will turn to the Lord because of the fear right now and many will find Him that never knew Him. Thank you, Lord—this is a good day! It is a remarkable day if there is but even one more added to those who belong to Him.

To God, a good day looks like the COVID-19! Yes, it was in my suffering that I first found Him. It has been in my suffering that I have turned to Him again and again. Yet, many blame God because they are blinded by the truth—many have turned away from Him in their suffering blaming Him for allowing this to happen, or they decide that there is No God and they reject Him. Don't blame God when we are the ones to blame. It is through our stubbornness, selfishness, idolatry that we choose to live for this world and push Him away. So, why would a good God if He is real, allow bad things to happen? You answer that—if you are questioning, the answer is right before you in what we call the Bible. Pick it up for once and read it. Pick it up for once and seek Him, you may be surprised that you will find Him. Seek and you will find, ask and the answers will be given, knock and that door is going to open. It is not a door of prosperity; it is a door that opens for eternal life. Remember, the false teachings today want us to find a god of this world, one that will fulfill all your dreams—a god that provides your heaven on earth. The main stream churches are too busy racking up money to build man's empires to worship man—not God!

However, the real God will never promise you the riches of this world—He will promise you a world beyond this one, one where there is never any sickness or disease, one where there is never any sadness nor hunger, one where there is only joy, love, and peace. We need to decide this day, do we choose heaven or do we choose this world?

Wake up America before it is too late!

CHAPTER FOUR
God's Mercy & Great Love

Here we are at the Mercy of God, the question has been asked, *"Why would a good God allow His people to go through hard times—why would He allow us to suffer, feel pain—why would He allow those who proclaim they belong to Him to die tragic deaths—to die at such an early age—to die and leave behind those who love and depend on them?"* Yes, there are so many, *"whys,"* and most of us have probably asked the question—but, have we heard the answer?

God is love; He is the definition of love. He does not love the way that man loves. His love is not conditional—yes, He loves us even though we do not deserve His love. Then why does He allow hardship in our lives? If God is love and He has mercy for mankind—forgiveness for those who do not deserve it, why does a forgiving, loving Father allow us to suffer through hardships?

To understand His ways and His thoughts, we must understand His mercy and His great love.

Deuteronomy 7:9 (NKJV) "Therefore know that the LORD your God, He is God, the faithful God who keeps covenant and mercy for a thousand generations with those who love Him and keep His commandments."

This is for those who love Him, those who keep His commandments. God requires that we keep His commandments—He requires that we love Him. Yet, we cannot even fathom love when we do not know Him intimately. Without His love infiltrating our body, our very lives—we cannot follow His commandments for we will fall short.

Proverbs 3:3-4 (NKJV) "Let not mercy and truth forsake you; bind them around your neck, write them on the tablet of your heart, and so find favor and high esteem in the sight of God and man."

Truth ties in with mercy. Without truth, we can never understand mercy. Yes, we know that mercy is forgiveness—yet, in our humanly minds, forgiveness is many times selective. We forgive those we love, those we care about—and, other times we may forgive those who have touched our lives in some way. Yet, we seldom think outside the box because our thoughts are not His thoughts. I believe we could all think about instances in our lives where there are those who have hurt us in some way—those who have made decisions that we dared not agree with and have harbored resentment, unforgiveness. There are many out there today that have no mercy on our president—many may have felt they were slighted in the work place where they did not receive rewards that they felt they deserved. Many today have much resentment towards a *"good"* God that allowed a loved one to die. How many of us could have gone through what Job went through and still showed loyalty and love towards a God that could have prevented him from the losses he incurred?

I encourage everyone to study the book of Job. This book has been my assurance through many storms in my life, that there is a God—a God who has NOT forgotten His people. To summarize the book of Job, in the beginning, God allowed satan to do what he wished to all that Job had but he could not touch Job himself. In Job 1, satan took Job's property and his children—yet, we see the results from his initial losses in verse 22.

Job 1:22 (ESV) In all this Job did not sin or charge God with wrong.

How many of us can lose all that we have to include our children and still love God? Next, satan was allowed to attack Job's health. Okay, as if taking all my children was not enough—would we not be thinking, *"God, just take me out of this world—there is nothing further for me to continue to live."* Yet—were we placed on this earth to multiply and find our pleasures in this world? Were we placed on this earth for our own will and pleasures? Were we placed on this earth to build our own gods to worship—gods such as our love for entertainment, love for our riches that fill our homes, and I could go on and on, but the question is—why were we created? Was it not for God's pleasure?

Revelation 4:11 (KJV) Thou art worthy, O Lord, to receive glory and honour and power: for thou hast created all things, and for thy pleasure they are and were created.

Once Job was afflicted with sores from the sole of his feet to the crown of his head, his wife said to him, *"Do you still hold fast to your integrity? Curse God and die."* How many would have already been cursing God for their pain and loss? Yet, what was Job's reply to his wife?

Job 2:10 (ESV) But he said to her, "You speak as one of the foolish women would speak. Shall we receive good from God, and shall we not receive evil?" In all this Job did not sin with his lips.

As one of the foolish women, why is this? His ways and His thoughts—our ways are not His ways nor are our thoughts! The ways of this world are foolishness, for the world has never known Him. In John 17, Jesus prayed to His Father knowing that the time had come. I encourage everyone to read all of John 17. It is a heartfelt prayer not for the world but for those who belong to Jesus Christ—His followers and also for all those to come that would receive His words and follow in His ways—whose ways? Jesus' ways—the Father's ways—the ways and thoughts that the world does not know! Jesus prays to His Father for those who belong to Him. Who did Jesus pray for? He only prayed for those who are His, those following His ways. He states, *"I am praying for them. I am not praying for the world but for those whom you have given me, for they are yours."* Please, I encourage everyone to read John 17. It is not about claiming to be a Christian, the real question is, are you living and breathing the life of Jesus Christ? Do you really have that deep relationship with Him? If not, praise God that you are seeking because the time is nearer than it was before, and He is still on His throne looking down at the nations as they look up for their redemption. In all his agony, Job never faltered away from what he knew as truth. Job was a broken man, but sometimes it is a great place to be where you can hear the voice of God.

So, why would a good God have allowed Job to endure what he went through, after all, Job was a man of God? What follows next in Job are the three friends that come to give their thoughts on why God was allowing Job to go through such turmoil. This is just like the world. When anyone faces pain and hardship, you always have those trying to give you worldly advice on their thoughts. The world cannot know the right advice to give unless their advice is to lead you back to the Word of God. Job's friends, one by one, gave him bad advice feeling as though his sufferings were due to sin in his own life. Although, one of the three friends felt that part of his sufferings were due to God's desire to humble him which was partly true but not entirely. When we are faced with uncertainty, far too often, we run to the world for answers because God is not answering us immediately. Do you ever wonder why God does not always answer us immediately? Perhaps, He is waiting to see what our faith looks like. Maybe, He is waiting for the moment when we step aside from the world, realizing that the world does NOT have the answers—realizing that the world does not have the wisdom—realizing the world is NOT what we need in our lives at that moment. We should never be seeking the world for our answers because you will be led astray.

At this point, Job was a broken man. He wished that he had never been born; he wished that death would overtake him. I can relate to what he felt. It was through the book of Job that I was able to get solace when I faced my daughter's death. I too wished to die; I too felt there was no reason to continue in this life. This is grief, and I could go on and on with what grief looks like. It is a natural part of life. We are not exempt from grief, yet—in the midst of any storm, where you decide to turn for comfort will determine how you walk through this life. Many turn to others for their comfort;

some shut themselves in and become bitter and hateful; some turn to God because they understand that the world cannot bring about the comfort needed to walk through the pain. Grieving is a process and one can only come out on the other side alive—once again, when they seek the Creator that understands the emotions and pain of mankind. It was only through my seeking and striving to stay close to God that I was able to walk through the death of my daughter.

I will not go through the whole book of Job, but once again, I encourage all to study the book. God is God and we do not always know why He allows certain things to happen, but we do know that it is His plan. We do know that He sees what we cannot. There were reasons that Job went through what he did. There are reasons that we face the things we do. In the end, Job was a man of God—in the end, Job gained much wisdom and knowledge, and in the end, God restored Job with twice as much as he had before. Yet, remember that Job lived in the Old Testament times—a time of prosperity; we live in the New Testament times—a time of tribulation. If we truly desire to walk with Jesus Christ, it should never be about gaining the riches of this world—the riches of this world will lead many down the wrong pathway.

How can we understand God's thoughts and ways? Proverbs—the book of wisdom—God's wisdom, is a great place to begin to understand how He thinks. It is not—nor will it ever be what a man or woman thinks that proclaim Scripture falsely. This is why it is detrimental to your salvation to begin to understand Scripture. I spoke on knowledge and wisdom in chapter one, and briefly mentioned understanding. How do we come to understand why we go through certain elements in this life? As I said earlier, knowledge is gained by knowing—knowing His truth which can only be found in studying deeply the Word of God. Wisdom is gained by much time of deep study. As we come to know, we become wise in God's ways and His thoughts. So, how do we come to understand? Understanding is knowing why God allows hardship. Understanding is knowing why God allows suffering. Understanding is knowing why God allows death, pain, heartache, and COVID-19.

We cannot begin to understand until we begin to gain the wisdom of His mercy and His love. Today, all over our world, people who claim to be Christians and those who do not—they live their lives one alongside the other with little differences. We cannot begin to claim the title of a Christian when our lives do not stand out as those first disciples. We cannot begin to say we have mercy for others when we do not understand His mercy. We cannot begin to say that we love, when we do not know His great love.

Micah 6:8 (NKJV) "He has shown you, O man, what is good; and what does the LORD require of you but to do justly, to love mercy, and to walk humbly with your God?"

As true Christians, do we consider our ways? Do we consider every single day how we shall live? Do we rise each morning giving thanks to our Father? Do we seek Him in the morning and throughout the day? Are our lives infiltrated with His Words, or will we carry ourselves through this life full of the world's ways and full of the world's thoughts? Our warnings are filled in the pages throughout the Word of God. Will we strive in this life to gain His knowledge—His wisdom— and His understanding?

Galatians 6:7-8 (NKJV) "Do not be deceived, God is not mocked; for whatever a man sows, that he will also reap. ⁸For he who sows to his flesh will of the flesh reap corruption, but he who sows to the Sprit will of the Spirit reap everlasting life.

Do we spend time pouring into the things of the flesh, or is our time filled with pouring into the things of the Spirit?

1 John 4:16 (NKJV) And so we have known and believed the love that God has for us. God is love, and he who abides in love abides in God, and God in him.

This is His love—a love that we cannot know unless we truly know Him. We cannot know this love nor understand it unless there is a genuine relationship with Him—with Jesus Christ. He is love; you can claim you know love all you want—but, without a true relationship with Him—your love is merely the love that the world knows.

1 John 4:18 (NKJV) There is no fear in love; but perfect love casts out fear, because fear involves torment. But he who fears has not been made perfect in love.

What does this mean? With COVID-19, many today are living in fear and many more will come to know fear. Yet, God is love and in Him there is no fear. Why? Perfect love drives out fear. Meaning, He is perfect and when you have that intimate relationship with Him, your love is perfected in Him. This means that you do not fear death. You do not fear COVID-19. Does this mean you will not acquire the virus? No, that is not what it means. It means that your faith and trust is in Him and if you contract the virus and even if you die, you understand that it was your time to leave this world.

Let me emphasize something here before I go further. COVID-19 is very contagious, and we have been given direction of how to help contain this threat from spreading to the masses. Many have died and continue to die. By no means what I have stated implies that we are to trust God by walking out into the world living, as if there is no threat. We are told by those in authority to quarantine and by disobeying the authorities, you are in disobedience to God.

Romans 13:1-2 (ESV) Let every person be subject to the governing authorities. For there is no authority except from God, and those that exist have been instituted by God. [2]Therefore whoever resists the authorities resists what God has appointed, and those who resist will incur judgment.

The Scriptures tell us that we are to obey man's laws. Unless those laws pertain to breaking God's laws, I would say that we are subject to the laws of man. Shame on those churches out there who willingly disobey the Word of God by claiming that God wants their church to remain open. Truly, those men or women are merely trying to fill their own pocket books and fame in this world, as they disobey the Scriptures. It does not matter how great you may think YOUR faith is, shame on you as a Christian to expect every person you come in contact with to be subject to your reckless life. Compassion is a great thing as a true believer in Jesus Christ. I, too, desire to use this opportunity to spread truth—but, I would not dare even walk up to someone's door to share Jesus when they may not even know Him, nor have faith to believe. Yet, faith has nothing to do with this virus, if in fact, God has allowed it to infiltrate the world as we know it today.

We place way too much emphasis on this world. We come to love this world to the extreme that none of us really want to leave this world. I know myself that I am ready to leave whenever He deems it is my time—yet, I dare say that I really do not want to leave my daughters, my son-in-law, nor my grandchildren. However, with that being said—if He is ready for my time to end on this earth, I also know that He will always be there for those I dearly love. I choose not to live out my life in fear for anything. I have lived through many storms in my life and am very thankful that He has brought me through the storms, and I am also thankful for the storms.

I have written about many of my storms in this life, but I will only choose one to disclose. What I am about to say, has at times offended others, but it must be said. The hardest storm that I have had to endure in my life was the death of my 25-year-old daughter. I have briefly mentioned her death but at this time, I would like to share more details. She was my first child. I could go on and on speaking of her life, sharing her love and happiness, always thinking of others instead of herself, giving needlessly for those in need—she had a heart for others that never wavered and a love for God unknown to many. She was forgiving and loving. I used to look at her life and wish that I had just a small part of her inside of me. She was the *"wind beneath my wings,"* literally! She may never know that it was because of her death that I went on to proclaim—

unafraid and unashamed, my deep conviction of my love for Jesus Christ. It was because of her that I stepped out of my box and became the writer that God had called me to be many, many years ago. I had always known to be gifted by God but would never rise up to the occasion. It was because of her that I walked through my fears to be a public speaker. It was because of her that I gained the compassion for mankind that I had lacked so many times. It was because of her that I became bold enough to stand up for Jesus Christ in truth, even when opposed by the many. I say all of this was because of her, but in reality, who I am today was who I was called to be—yet, I would not step up to the plate. It was God allowing her to die that transformed my life in a positive way.

My daughter and I spent a considerable amount of time together only a few weeks before she was killed. In this time, she wept relentlessly. Why? Her tears were always about helping others and pleasing God. She had been crying out to God because she knew there was something that He wanted her to do, but He had not shown her. Yet, she felt His presence and knew there was a reason for her life. The story goes much further back than that particular day. It goes back through many trials, hard aches, and many storms. Months prior, she came close to dying where God had awakened me in the night to pray for her. She was living in Dallas and I had no idea what was happening, but I got out of bed and began to pray. I will not go into the details on that story, but fast forward to the day she cried to me as she had been seeking Him, it was only a few weeks later that she was killed. Why? Yes, my question to God was why? *"God, why did you awaken me months prior to pray for her? God, why did you not awaken me this time? God, why did she cry to me just a few weeks ago knowing that You had a purpose for her life and then you allowed her to die?"* God is a most awesome God for He will give you your answers when you seek Him. My answers came and there were many, but the main one that I want to share is that her purpose was *"me."*

I was my daughter's main purpose in this life. Yes, there were many of her friends that turned to Jesus after this and almost 20 years later, I am still hearing from her friends that have not forgotten her and have continued to turn to Jesus. Yet, when I was pregnant with my daughter at a very young age, my mother had died. I won't go into all the details, but I had nothing to live for, so I thought. My life was horrible. My father had remarried a woman 20 years younger and no longer had need for me or my sister in his life. I found myself at 17, alone having lost both parents, being given a choice to either have an abortion or marry the father to the baby. Her dad was a severe alcoholic and abusive. I won't go into all the details there because I love his family very deeply—a very loving and kind family. However, I found myself desolate. I was lost and felt that the only way out was suicide. I would spend days at my mother's grave telling her that as soon as I gave birth to my baby, I planned to end my life. I felt that was the best way. I knew that my baby would have a good life, as the first grandchild to her dad's parents, they were pretty awesome people.

Yet, God always has a better plan. When I gave birth and held my daughter in my arms to breast feed her, I can still see her little tiny eyes as they looked into mine that first day. I fell totally in love knowing for the first time what it was like to love and what it was like for someone to love me unconditionally. The love of a child is the closest we can ever get to understanding the love of God, as it is unconditional. When my daughter died, I wanted to die. Yet, I could not take my life, but I did pray for God to take me because the pain was so great. However, her death was the beginning of a life that I had yet to discover. There were many things which happened from those years where God was conditioning me for who He had called me to be. It was because of her death that I became who God called me to be. What I wanted to say that has offended others, understanding God's ways, if I was given the chance to go back and stop my daughter's death, would I? No, I would never choose to bring her back. Her death was part of God's plan. Her death transformed my life and many others, but the other part is that I know she is in heaven. If she is in heaven and that is our final destination as a Christian—if heaven is greater than our lives on earth, why would we want to bring someone back to earth? Why would I want to take her from heaven to have her be put back on earth with its suffering and pain? My hope is that when my time is near, He will take me and I accept that knowing that He will still be here with my other daughters, my son-in-law, and grandchildren.

There are storms in this world all around us. I am not talking about natural storms but spiritual storms. It is the same thing with the coronavirus. So, why is it that a good God would allow His people to suffer? Why would He allow many to die from this dreadful virus? If God is a God of love and mercy, why do His people suffer? His people, who are His people? God knows those who are truly His. He knows those who are striving to walk out this walk. He knows those who are seeking Him, and He also knows those who are living out in this world in sin because they know no other way. God is a compassionate God, and He desires that we follow Him—not this world. He desires that His people come together in one accord like never before. God is building His church today—His church that no man can separate. It is not a building—it is a people—those who are willing to let go of this world and share the true gospel to those lost in the world, those who continue to seek for something far greater than they have ever known. These—the lost, many dare not walk into the buildings that we call church, many dare not seek out the god of this world because all they have seen is the corruption within the churches today. Why would those that are lost in this world desire that which looks no different than the world? Let me clarify once more, this is not all the churches today—yet, the true churches are the few and many times hard to find. Yet, those who are hurting and really desire something they can trust and believe in—these will never buy into what is proclaimed by the majority of the churches today. These do not desire the riches of man, they only desire something greater than this world has ever offered them. These are the lowly of the world—the humble.

I can truthfully say that over the last six or seven years, God has led me across paths of the lowly, the humble. They dare not infiltrate the so-called churches today because they do not see the God of the Bible. They do not desire to associate with the Pharisees. Yet, there are amazing churches out there that are striving to get the true gospel of Jesus Christ out to those seeking truth. These churches are hard to find. Yet, they can be found but many times, they can only be found through connections on the web.

CHAPTER FIVE
Trusting in a Good God in Your Storm

Psalm 28:7 (ESV) The Lord is my strength and my shield; in him my heart trusts, and I am helped; my heart exults, and with my song I give thanks to him.

How do we let go of our fears and quieten our mind? It begins with your heart. Of course, this is never referring to the physical heart but the spiritual. God is a spiritual being and being created in His image, we too have a spirit. I will not go into deep detail but I do teach extensively on the aspects of man in much greater clarity. However, what I want to draw upon, is that we are spirit, soul, and body.

1 Thessalonians 5:23 (ESV) Now may the God of peace himself sanctify you completely, and may your whole spirit and soul and body be kept blameless at the coming of our Lord Jesus Christ.

Your soul is the person you are on the inside. It is your individual makeup. Your soul is your personality, your thoughts, your talents—your soul defines the person that you are. Your spirit is in constant battle over your body for your soul. When we all leave this world, our body decays into dust returning to the earth.

Ecclesiastes 12:7 (ESV) and the dust returns to the earth as it was, and the spirit returns to God who gave it.

Your soul will not die—who you are on the inside will not die.

Matthew 10:28 (ESV) And do not fear those who kill the body but cannot kill the soul. Rather fear him who can destroy both soul and body in hell.

Powerful—there is nothing that can kill your soul, but God can destroy both your body and your soul by allowing *"your eternity"* to be spent in hell. The opposite—if we fear God by obeying His laws, you will see heaven and your soul will live on likewise. In other words, it will never be about trying to preserve your life here on earth but about living your life righteously in order that you make heaven. Anyone or anything (COVID-19) can kill the body, but it will be up to God whether you make heaven or hell.

Regarding our makeup, I like to refer to it this way—we are a spiritual being, which was the breath of life given to each of us by our Creator. We have a soul which defines each of us individually, and we temporarily live in a body. Yet, the body or our flesh is continually at war against our spirit.

Galatians 5:16-17 (ESV) But I say, walk by the Spirit, and you will not gratify the desires of the flesh. For the desires of the flesh are against the Spirit, and the desires of the Spirit are against the flesh, for these are opposed to each other, to keep you from doing the things you want to do.

Now, going back to our fears—learning how to quieten our mind where our heart is right with God. So, how do we let go of our fears? How to we fully trust in the Lord with our whole heart? Jesus tells us that everything that comes out of our mouth proceeds from our heart.

Matthew 15:16-20a (ESV) And he said, "Are you also still without understanding? Do you not see that whatever goes into the mouth proceeds from the heart, and this defiles a person. [19]For out of the heart come evil thoughts, murder, adultery, sexual immorality, theft, false witness, slander. [20]These are what defile a person."

We cannot begin to let go of our fears, worries, hate, anger, if in fact, our heart is not right with God. If you read all of Matthew 15, Jesus was clearly teaching His disciples that it was not about the food we eat that defiles a person. In those days, there were particular foods that were not to be eaten. What He was trying to clarify that it was not what went into the mouth that defiled a person but what went into the heart. Remember, food goes into the stomach and is dispelled. What we choose to read, watch, and listen to in this world, those are the things which go into the heart. When we spend countless hours feeding the world into our heart—it will be those things which proceed out of our mouth in words, thoughts, etc.

In Psalm 28 at the beginning of this chapter, the psalmist trust in all aspects of his life rests in the Lord. We cannot begin to trust in the Lord when our heart is filled with the world. To walk through any storm with our Creator by our side, will take a people who are willing to separate their minds from this world. It will take filling our heart with more and more of Him by deep study in His Word where He will clean up our heart to be pure, as more and more of the world is pushed out.

A quick story that I have shared many times. It was during my days that God had separated me from the world for 6 months. I poured into Him and He poured into me with knowledge and wisdom. I teach many times on the storms in our lives, relating a spiritual storm to a natural storm. Perhaps, in understanding the relation will encourage us to let go of our worries, seek Him to a greater degree, and let go of this world while walking close to Him—as He fills us with trust and faith.

Storms come and go in the natural and in the spiritual. Jesus tells us in this life we will have tribulation, but He also tells us to take heart because He has overcome this world. *(John 16:33)*

There are always reasons for storms. Briefly, I taught a lesson many years ago and have written about one such storm several times. This particular storm happened in 1883. It began with a volcanic eruption that sunk two thirds of the Krakatau Island located in the Indonesian province of Lampung. Tens of thousands of lives were lost, as there were also tsunamis that followed this eruption. The massive amount of material deposited by this natural disaster dramatically altered the ocean floor surrounding the island and significantly increased the land mass of its neighboring islands. In 1927, there was another eruption that once again took away land mass from the Island of Krakatau and created another smaller island that they called Anak Krakatau, which meant child of Krakatau. If you would like to read about these natural disasters, you can google Krakatau eruption of 1883 and Krakatau eruption of 1927. There are several accounts written on both of these. Please note, the spelling is frequently noted as Krakatoa, but the correct spelling is Krakatau. Recently, while writing this book—once again, Krakatau is in the news as there have been new eruptions. I have been teaching on this island form many, many years—hearing once again of its eruptions, assures me that the Lord uses these illustrations to help us perceive greater clarity of storms as they relate in the natural but also in the spiritual.

A natural storm helps us to be able to understand spiritual storms. In a spiritual storm when we are going through a tough time, we seldom stop to think that just maybe God is doing a work in our lives and the outcome will all be worth it. For the natural disaster, because of the storms or eruptions, there were things taken away and things added. The neighboring islands gained more land mass and Krakatau had less land mass. In 1927, a whole new island was created and named as the child of the original island. Looking at this in a spiritual sense, we come to the Lord to change our lives, and we really get more than we bargained for. Not understanding how God works, we murmur and complain because we fail to understand. In our storms, God is merely removing things that need to be removed and adding things that need to be added. God sometimes will remove things in the natural and sometimes even things spiritually that are not of Him. He also adds things that need to be added. As God is doing a work in us, when we submit to Him and just trust Him, it will not take 40 years like it did the Israelites. When we trust the work that He is doing in us, one day we will awaken and realize that we are a child of God just as Anak Krakatau is a child of Krakatau.

Proverbs 3:5 (ESV) Trust in the Lord with all your heart, and do not lean on your own understanding.

As we draw closer to our Lord and Savior, we gradually allow the Holy Spirit to do a work in us as He removes those things in our lives and replaces them with more and more of Him. When we strive to live our lives daily—filling ourselves with His Words, our heart becomes purer daily. When our heart begins to line up with His Words, our trust also begins to rely on Him and not on this world or not on man.

Isaiah 26:3 (ESV) You keep him in perfect peace whose mind is stayed on you, because he trusts in you.

Matthew 6:25 (ESV) "Therefore I tell you, do not be anxious about your life, what you will eat or what you will drink, nor about your body, what you will put on. Is not life more than food, and the body more than clothing?"

Psalm 9:10 (ESV) And those who know your name put their trust in you, for you, O Lord, have not forsaken those who seek you.

CHAPTER SIX
Rejoice, Today is a Good Day

Psalm 47:8 (ESV) God reigns over the nations; God sits on his holy throne.

Yes, today is a good day because God still reigns over all the nations; He still sits on His holy throne!

Why would a good God allow the coronavirus, COVID-19? Why would He allow pain and suffering?

Psalm 46:10 (ESV) "<u>Be still</u>, and know that I am God. <u>I will be exalted among the nations, I will be exalted in the earth</u>!"

This life, this world is NOT about us; it is about Him and it has always been about Him. BE STILL—what better way of getting our attention than for catastrophe to happen, or—perhaps we should use the phrase, *"when all hell breaks loose!"* Of course, that is man's term not God's. When all *"hell"* breaks loose, we do not even have a clue what that really looks like. Praise God there are trials—tests—storms—catastrophes—none of these things that happen today will ever even come close to what life would look like in hell! Praise God and rejoice that there are storms like the COVID-19 to awaken His people to *"be still"* and know He is God—*"be still"* and know that these sufferings today are only temporary but the suffering to come—eternal suffering in hell, nothing you have ever known will compare to eternity in hell.

Yes, God is a most awesome, loving God because He allows for the pain—He allows the suffering—He allows the storms, tests, trials—to awaken His people to turn back to Him. He desires that we love Him, not a man-made love, but genuine love that awakens every morning saying, *"Lord, this is Your day—I am your son or your daughter—my life is in Your hands, let my time not be wasted striving for the riches of this world, striving for fame and fortune, striving to acquire all this world has to offer, striving to be a friend to the world—let my time be used wisely, filled with Your presence—filled with Your Word—Your Truth—let my life glorify you in everything I do!"*

Why did Job go through everything he did? Why would God allow Job, a man of God—one whose life was lived honoring Him to go through his suffering? Perhaps, we can understand why those living out in the world not honoring God would go through storms, but why Job? This speaks for any who claim to be Christians. There are different people in the world today—those who walk with the Lord and do not deny Him; those who perhaps in words claim they believe in Him, yet their lives are lived as the world; those who openly deny Him; those who neither think one way or the other but live just as the world. The majority today to include the Christian population live just as the world. There are little differences. They go about their lives striving to place their mark on this world—working, gaining riches, enjoying the pleasures of this world—yet, a true Christian is not one in name only, but one who is willing to walk away from any and everything that is contrary to the Word of God. A true Christian is one that needs not the pleasures of this world—one that does not desire the popularity of the world—one that does not desire the riches of this world—one that will suffer, be persecuted, be hated because they have come to understand *(there's that word again-*

understand) that there is something far greater than this world. It is those who are willing to lose everything in order to gain heaven.

Mark 8:35 (ESV) For whoever would save his life will lose it, but whoever loses his life for my sake and the gospel's will save it.

Philippians 3:7-8 (ESV) But whatever gain I had, I counted as loss for the sake of Christ. [8]Indeed, I count everything as loss because of the surpassing worth of knowing Christ Jesus my Lord. For his sake I have suffered the loss of all things and count them as rubbish, in order that I may gain Christ. [9]and be found in him, not having a righteousness of my own that comes from the law, but that which comes through faith in Christ, the righteousness from God that depends on faith—[10]that I may know him and the power of his resurrection, and may share his sufferings, becoming like him in death, [11]that by any means possible I may attain the resurrection from the dead.

There are times in our walk that we need reminders. No matter where you are in your walk with Jesus Christ, we all need those reminders to know that He is still on His throne—He is still in charge! Job's storms were allowed not because of anything he had done wrong— but a reminder in the good times, as well as in those times of uncertainty, we never take our eyes off of Jesus. Job's storms taught him valuable lessons, lessons that we always need reminders—here he was, in the midst of his storms, what happened? To begin with, many voices came in to give Job advice—those of his friends! We see this every day—we all do. When we or our family and friends are going through hard times, everyone wants to give them advice. It is in those hard times, more than anything, we should be running to God for His advice. I'm not saying that people will always give bad advice but as Christians, the only advice we need is in the Word of God. Yes, it is alright to be comforted by others, but ultimately, we run to Jesus Christ not to man. We run to God not to this world.

Is today a good day to the Lord? Yes, it is a glorious day when the world as we know it has shut down. It is a glorious day when the nightclubs, the bars, the strip clubs, all entertainment has seized, sports, recreation, and the churches have all shut down! Yes, I included the churches or rather I have included the buildings, for we are the church! God wants a people that look up to Him—cry out to Him. He desires that we seek Him individually. Well, here we have it—the churches are shut down, as well! Do we stop being the church? No—we use this opportunity wherever we are today, in our homes, to look up to the heavens and cry out to a God that desires His people seek Him directly. Today has made history—tomorrow will also make history! It is what we do today that will determine our tomorrow. What you determine your life to look like, will determine your tomorrow. God is still on His throne, and He still desires that none should perish.

In our world, we all look at a good day as everything going well in our lives. Our day at school or work is filled with peace. Our friends and family do not say anything or do anything that would take away that peace. At school, everything goes smoothly, and at work, there is no conflict that causes strife, worry, anger, etc. Yes, I know everyone wants days that run smoothly where everyone likes us, loves us, caters to us, befriends us, sides with us during conflicts, makes us feel good about ourselves, etc. We also want days where our money is sufficient; all our needs are met; we have no contentions; things go our way always; we have enough food to eat well, pay our bills, have more than enough to buy all our wants besides our needs; our friends stick by our side; our spouses cater to us, they love only us, they never make mistakes, they never cheat, they never insult us, they never ridicule us; our parents never chastise us, discipline us; and I could go on and on and on with the list. I think you get what I mean. If our days went exactly as we willed them, we would say at the end of that day, *"Yes, today was a good day."* However, welcome to the real world. We all know that our days are not going to go as we would wish them. Our days may be good at times and other times, things happen—things happen and that is just the way it is, or is it?

Again, *"Why would a God, <u>if He were real</u>, allow me to go through this?"*

I am sure rather you are a believer or unsure that God is real, you have asked yourself that same question. Myself, I have had plenty of times to ask that question, if I had so desired. I have certainly gone through many things in my life that someone would have probably asked, *"Why do you believe in a God that has allowed you to suffer so many times?"* Yes, my daughter's death was the storm of all storms, but hey—God watched His Son as He was beaten, flogged, nails hammered into his hands and feet, ridiculed, spit on, etc. Should we just accept our pain because God had to also watch Jesus being crucified?

When my daughter died, before she was even buried, I cried out to God, in my time alone, saying, *"I will never blame you for this—I will never stop loving you for this, but I just want to know why."* He began to show me the reasons slowly over the years that followed, and today, I totally understand why there are times of suffering.

Before closing this book, the Lord showed me something that I believe will really minster to a lot of people. I have been fortunate that I have understood the Lord's voice in my own life and have recognized it as such for many, many years. Yet, I feel that there are those out there that are looking for that audible voice coming down from heaven. His voice is not audible. His voice is a still small voice normally heard from deep within.

1 King 19:11-12 (NKJV) Then he said, "Go out, and stand on the mountain before the LORD." And behold, the LORD passed by, and a great and strong wind tore into the mountains and broke the rocks in pieces before the LORD, but the LORD was not in the wind; and after the wind an earthquake, but the LORD was not in the earthquake; [12]And after the earthquake a fire, but the LORD was not in the fire; and after the fire a still small voice."

If you continue the story in 1 King, you will learn that the still small voice, other translations say a low whisper, was the Lord's voice. Many times, we cannot hear His voice due to all the chaos in our lives. The chaos are the storms which produce the wind, earthquakes, and fires. This does not mean that He is not speaking; it means that He is still speaking but we are unable to hear Him. Sometimes, we must quieten the storms. How exactly do we do that? If God allows the storms in our lives and it is because of the storms that we cannot hear His voice, then how are we to quieten them when He allowed them? It has never been about trying to quieten the storms in our lives. It has always been about walking close to Jesus Christ during any and all storms. You alone cannot quieten the storms, but you can learn how to walk through them. You can learn how to not focus on the storms but keep your eyes on Him—your Creator. He is there and has always been there. Are we not told that He will never forsake us? *(Deuteronomy 31:6-8, Hebrews 13:5-6, Isaiah 41:10-13, 1 Chronicles 28:20)*

When you are steadily seeking Him through His Word, you are going to hear Him, but it may not be in a way that your mind interprets. I want to give you an example of how He communicates and will do so as it pertains to this book, please follow me on this—

I hear my granddaughter in her prayers daily say, "— and, God let Mommy have a good day; let Gammy have a good day; let Sissy have a good day; let everyone have a good day—"

Me: I begin to silently say to God, *"I know that what she perceives as a good day is that everything goes well— according to what we expect, but God—that is not how You look at our life."*

The Small Voice: *"If you were to pray for what you perceived as a good day, what would that look like?"*

Me: *"It would be where everything went according to my plans—nothing bad happened."*

The Small Voice: *"If everyone received what they wished for, would they ever have need to seek me?"*

Me: *"No, but so many never seek you anyway."*

The Small Voice: *"That may be true, but do you remember when your daughter died?"*

Me: *"How could I ever forget."*

The Small Voice: *"How did it change your life?"*

Me: *"I can't even begin to name the extent of how it changed my life."*

The Small Voice: *"Do you remember all the other times when you had strayed away or you were not spending as much time studying My Word, how it took something that you would have considered a bad day to awaken you to return."*

Me: *"Yes, all those other times, I became distracted with this world and staying too busy that I slacked on spending time with you."*

The Small Voice: *"Would you had rather that I not have allowed those bad days where your days here on earth could have been considered good?"*

Me: *"No, I can't imagine my life without You—without the wisdom and knowledge I have gained through the storms of life—without the understanding that I have finally gained perspective."*

The Small Voice: *"What about all the times you prayed for your daughters to return to me—when I allowed the chaos in their lives, was I not answering your prayers?"*

Me: *"Yes, and you still do today."*

The Small Voice: *"What about all the times that I have allowed you to not get the things you wanted in this life, do your regret not having those things of this world?"*

Me: *"No Father, you are more than enough."*

The Small Voice: *"Do you remember the time where I placed you in a particular position at a church for a season and it was a few years later before you understood why?"*

Me: *"Yes Lord, I heard Your voice for several weeks telling me that I was going to be placed in that position. Yet, I did not understand why until much later."*

The Small Voice: *"Do you remember after I had you walk away from that church because I had another plan?"*

Me: *"Of course, it was a hard decision because I had many friends."*

The Small Voice: *"Yet, you trusted me and walked away. Do you remember the pain when the church turned on you and let all your friends know that they could no longer be your friend because you walked away?"*

Me: *"Yes, it was very painful."*

The Small Voice: *"Was I there for you during that time?"*

Me: *"Yes, you were all I had."*

The Small Voice: *"What did I ask you during that time of your pain—when you wanted to go back to the church because you felt like you had lost everything?"*

Me: *"You asked me—if I were to lose everything—family, friends, my position as a leader, where all I had left was You—was that not enough?"*

God was and still is enough today! I faced my storm for 6 months—6 months with no friends, no family, just myself and God. I refer to it as my time in my desert with God—yet, it was the most awesome time in my life. It was a time of great growth—a time of intimacy where I began to understand His ways and His thoughts. Yes, the loss of my daughter was the greatest hardship I have ever endured, but the 6 months in my desert brought me to a level of understanding that I am not sure I would have gained, if I had not endured that particular storm. I wanted to share this because I want others to know that His voice carries on conversations with you from your spirit deep within.

This is Biblical, He was enough yesterday and He is still enough today. Walking with the Lord is a relationship and if you want this bad enough, He is no respecter of persons. Get His Word down on the inside of you. Read, study, and then study again. Speak to Him and listen because He is speaking back. Please know that it is alright to step out and be different. Those who are willing to let go of this world as we know it and sacrifice their lives for the sake of Christ may very well lose much, but in the end, they will gain much.

John 15:18-19 (ESV) "If the world hates you, know that it has hated me before it hated you. [19]If you were of the world, the world would love you as its own; but because you are not of the world, but I chose you out of the world, therefore the world hates you.

A prayer that Jesus prayed to His Father—

John 17:14-19 (ESV) "I have given them your word, and the world has hated them because they are not of the world, just as I am not of the world. [15]I do not ask that you take them out of the world, but that you keep them from the evil one. [16]They are not of the world, just as I am not of the world. [17]Sanctify them in the truth; your word is truth. [18]As you sent me into the world, so I have sent them into the world. [19]And for their sake I consecrate myself, that they also may be sanctified in truth.

1 John 2:15-17 (ESV) Do not love the world or the things in the world. If anyone loves the world, the love of the Father is not in him. [16]For all that is in the world—the desires of the flesh and the desires of the eyes and pride of life—is not from the Father but is from the world. [17]And the world is passing away along with its desires, but whoever does the will of God abides forever.

James 4:4 (ESV) You adulterous people! Do you not know that friendship with the world is enmity with God? Therefore whoever wishes to be a friend of the world makes himself an enemy of God.

Romans 12:2 (ESV) Do not be conformed to this world, but be transformed by the renewal of your mind, that by testing you may discern what is the will of God, what is good and acceptable and perfect.

Is God enough? Is He enough today in our lives or do we desire to have both—the riches of this world, friendship with the world, the acceptance of this world, or God?

So, what do most people believe a good day looks like to the Lord? I would assume that most people have never even considered the question. Most people are too busy considering their own thoughts instead of what the Bible tells us. Or, most Christians are considering what they have been taught from the pulpit which again, is what a man or woman has imparted to them from the pulpit—books—articles, etc. Well, I have only asked my granddaughter that question, *"What do you think a good day to the Lord looks like,"* so I am unsure what your answers may be.

With our world in an uproar, running here and there—scrambling to get people to their homes—school closures—N95 masks to hospitals—more ventilators needed than can be made—National Guard called into many cities—governments spending countless hours, little sleep discussing solutions—hospital beds being filled—grocery stores exhausting every resource and trying to get trucks in daily to meet people's needs—the masses either off work with no pay or less pay—headlines continuing across the globe with the cases continually increasing, the death toll rising—quarantines being issued—stay at home orders—stimulus packages being voted on—pleadings for more supplies—triage tents being set up for make shift hospitals—talks of choosing those who can get into hospitals and those that will be turned away because of lack of beds, staffing, ventilators, etc.

Currently, what our world looks like today, does NOT look like a good day. What happened? Did God forget about us? I mean, after all, America alone has always been a blessed country, so why would a good God allow this chaos to happen in America? Sometimes, we can understand this for other countries, but America? I mean, we have churches in the south almost in every neighborhood, right? We have ministries—huge ministries all over America and some of those have even expanded out through other countries. Why, it seems like America is a good neighbor, right? We are always helping other countries, why would a good God allow this to happen to America?

Remember, His ways and His thoughts are not our thoughts. So, why has a good God allowed this to happen?

Storms build faith—endurance. Storms grow us to maturity of which we must be fully matured, they teach us valuable lessons where we gain wisdom-through years of storms, we gain understanding that can only happen as we grow, growing only happens through maturity—we learn how He thinks—we learn His ways—we learn what true love looks like—not worldly love. God's love looks to eternity not for today.

Luke 21:28 (KJV) And when these things begin to come to pass, then look up, and lift up your heads; for your redemption draweth nigh.

Haggai 1:5 (NKJV) Now therefore, thus says the LORD of hosts: "Consider your ways!"

Joshua 24:15 (NKJV) "And if it seems evil to you to serve the LORD, choose for yourselves this day whom you will serve, whether the gods which your fathers served that were on the other side of the River, or the gods of the Amorites, in whose land you dwell. But as for me and my house, we will serve the LORD."

References

Chapter Three
Wake Up America

1. Commentary on the New Testament, by Charles Spurgeon.

www.ingramcontent.com/pod-product-compliance
Lightning Source LLC
Chambersburg PA
CBHW052117110526
44592CB00013B/1643